THE ETHICAL LEADERSHIP HANDBOOK

DAY DEVOTIONAL

THE ETHICAL LEADERSHIP HANDBOOK

© 2013 Aimee Colbert, Fort Worth, TX

All rights reserved. No part of this book may be reproduced or transmitted in any form or by any means without written permission from the author.

About the author

Aimee Colbert is changing the way that Christians view mental and emotional wellness. She has been training, educating, teaching and reaching thousands with her messages of goal setting, mental health, relationship building and purpose.

Aimee's distinctive point of view is a direct result of past tragedies that has produced a present day triumph after growing up poor, being a victim of domestic violence and a Katrina survivor.

Between 2006-present, Aimee has been speaking before churches, businesses, governmental programs, organizations, schools and universities throughout Texas.

In 2008 Aimee Colbert became an ordained minister and launched her first ministry. She went on to become a drug/alcohol counselor, educator, activist and author.

Aimee has been the regional spokesperson for many groups and organizations. She is a noted conference speaker and guest lecturer. She has appeared on cable programs such as S.P.I.C.E.S., Manna Express, and The Bible Says. She is often contacted by national news journalist to comment on social matters.

Aimee hosted a live call in radio program on Christian social issues. She has become a sought after public speaker and lecturer. Aimee is gifted with an extraordinary view of relationships and Christian life.

Author Aimee Colbert is a mental health advocate and theoretician. Aimee practices as a Pastoral counselor in Fort Worth, TX.

She offers therapeutic sessions, training workshops and relationship education courses. Aimee assists individuals who are interested in overcoming habits, goal setting, problem-solving, relationship building and purpose discovery.

Aimee is currently a board member of "The Essence of a Woman Summit" and "Kingdom Living Center Church". She is also a guest writer for "Modern Christian Women", "View from The Pew" and "Shalom Magazine".

Aimee Colbert is the author of The Irreplaceable Woman, The Drama Free Life, Dear Carlos, To Be A Man of God, Aimee's Advice, I'm Just Sayin Vol 1&2, You're Stupid & Shallow So Stay Single Ya Dummy, The Irreplaceable Man and I Survived which discusses the social issues that affect us all and that bind us together.

Noted for her quick wit, vigorous debate and enlightening oratory, Aimee is a challenge to the opposition and an instructive persuasive counselor to allies.

THE ETHICAL LEADER

The idea that a leader is simply the person in charge or the person that commands someone to undertake a task is diminishing. Today the world requires an ethical leader and an ethical leader is a nurturing leader. This person not only possesses leadership qualities but has the ability to transform their subordinate's views. They can also inspire and motivate them. This takes "Emotional Intelligence".

The ethical leader has emotional intelligence…

Emotional intelligence is the ability to be aware of your emotions, flaws, etc. but most importantly, how these things affect those around you. Emotional intelligence requires you to be aware of the feelings of others. This means that you will have to increase your level of empathy. This is how we build and maintain ethical standards.

Everyone loves people with EI because they are easy to work with and are a great addition to any team. The reason why is because they make others feel good. When they do this, people are readily too willing to show appreciation for meeting their needs. Do you have good EI?

Characteristics of Emotional Intelligence

Daniel Goleman, an American psychologist, developed a structure to define what it means to have EI:

1. Self-Awareness – People with high emotional intelligence are usually very self-aware. They understand their emotions, and because of this, they don't let their feelings rule them. They're confident – because they trust their intuition and don't let their emotions get out of control.

They're also willing to take an honest look at themselves. They know their strengths and weaknesses, and they work on these areas so they can perform better. Many people believe that this self-awareness is the most important part of emotional intelligence.

2. Self-Regulation – This is the ability to control emotions and impulses. People who self-regulate typically don't allow themselves to become too angry or jealous, and they don't make impulsive, careless decisions. They think before they act. Characteristics of self-regulation are thoughtfulness, comfort with change, integrity, and the ability to say no.

3. Motivation – People with a high degree of emotional intelligence are usually motivated. They're willing to defer immediate results for long-term success. They're highly productive, love a challenge, and are very effective in whatever they do.

4. Empathy – This is perhaps the second-most important element of emotional intelligence. Empathy is the ability to identify with and understand the wants, needs, and viewpoints of those around you. People with empathy are good at recognizing the feelings of others, even when those feelings may not be obvious. As a result, empathetic people are usually excellent at managing relationships, listening, and relating to others. They avoid stereotyping and judging too quickly, and they live their lives in a very open, honest way.

5. Social Skills – It's usually easy to talk to and like people with good social skills, another sign of high emotional intelligence. Those with strong social skills are typically team players. Rather than focus on their own success first, they help others develop and shine. They can manage disputes, are excellent communicators, and are masters at building and maintaining relationships.

As you've probably determined, emotional intelligence can be a key to success in your life – especially in your relationship. The ability to manage relationships is very important, so developing and using your emotional intelligence can be a good way to show others the positivity inside of you.

How to recognize if you have low EI:

☐ Poor impulse control

☐ Inability to focus

☐ Pessimistic

☐ Disrespectful

☐ General unhappiness with self

☐ Aggressive

- ☐ Fearful

- ☐ Over-reactive

- ☐ Lack of empathy

- ☐ Mistrustful

- ☐ Destructive

- ☐ Floods with anxiety

- ☐ Non-assertive

- ☐ falls apart under stress

- ☐ Sulky

- ☐ Seeks immediate gratification

- ☐ Uncaring

- ☐ chronically sad or angry

- ☐ Impolite, rude

- ☐ Preoccupied with negativity

- ☐ Passive

- ☐ Emotionally inappropriate

- ☐ Whiny

- ☐ Overly sensitive to criticism

How to Improve Your Emotional Intelligence

The good news is that emotional intelligence CAN be taught and developed. Many books and tests are available to help you determine your current EI, and identify where you may need to do some work. You can also use these tips:

• Observe how you react to people. Do you rush to judgment before you know all of the facts? Do you stereotype? Look honestly at how you think and interact with other people. Try to put yourself in their place, and be more open and accepting of their perspectives and needs.

•Look at your work environment. Do you seek attention for your accomplishments? Humility can be a wonderful quality, and it doesn't mean that you're shy or lack self-confidence. When you practice humility, you say that you know what you did, and you can be quietly confident about it. Give others a chance to shine – put the focus on them, and don't worry too much about getting praise for yourself.

•Do a self-evaluation. What are your weaknesses? Are you willing to accept that you're not perfect and that you could work on some areas to make yourself a better person? Have the courage to look at yourself honestly – it can change your life.

- Examine how you react to stressful situations. Do you become upset every time there's a delay or something doesn't happen the way you want? Do you blame others or become angry at them, even when it's not their fault? The ability to stay calm and in control in difficult situations is highly valued – in the business world and outside it. Keep your emotions under control when things go wrong.

- Take responsibility for your actions. If you hurt someone's feelings, apologize directly – don't ignore what you did or avoid the person. People are usually more willing to forgive and forget if you make an honest attempt to make things right.

- Examine how your actions will affect others – before you take those actions. If your decision will impact others, put yourself in their place. How will they feel if you do this? Would you want that experience? If you must take the action, how can you help others deal with the effects?

The Traits of an Ethical Leader

The ethical leader shows ambition, competency, individuality, equality, integrity, service, responsibility, accuracy, respect, dedication, diversity, improvement, enjoyment/fun, loyalty, credibility, honesty, innovativeness, teamwork, excellence, accountability, empowerment, quality, efficiency, dignity, collaboration, stewardship, empathy, accomplishment, courage, wisdom, independence, security, challenge, influence, learning, compassion, friendliness, discipline/order, generosity, persistency, optimism, dependability, and flexibility.

Leaders are made, they are not born. They are made by hard effort, which is the price which all of us must pay to achieve any goal that is worthwhile.
~ Vince Lombardi

CHALLENGES TO YOUR ETHICS

When dealing with suppliers, 86% of senior executives say a lack of ethical standards would be enough to not do business with a supplier.

~Doremus/Financial Times, October 2005

Think about these business ethics scenarios that happen in organizations and businesses from time to time.

- A manager ships items that he knows is damaged but assumes the customer won't notice.

- A sales rep lies to customers about his being a user of the products he's selling.

- An executive uses private company leads to gain leads for their own side business.

- A company lies about the quality of an item to sell it.

- An employee steals office supplies.

- An employee has an office affair.

- A financial officer is misappropriating funds despite instructions from those above them.

- A financial officer tells a contractor that their "check is in the mail" when he knows he hasn't written the check.

- A sales rep flirts with customers when they come to ask him about products or services.

Those were a few examples of how some people compromise their integrity on bigger issues but now I want to list a few scenarios that we are all faced with on the job on a more daily basis.

- You are using the company restroom and use up the last roll of toilet paper, or the last piece of paper towel and return back to your department without addressing the issue.

- You call in sick to your supervisor because you want to have the day off to have fun.

- You decide not to clean up a mess you made in the break room because no one was there and you have more important things to do.

- You call in after commiting to showing up or you show up without letting anyone know but then blame someone else for the mistake.

- You tell potential customers, employees or contractors that you can do something for them but when they pursue it and find out what you said wasn't true, you pretend that they misinterpreted you.

- You withhold your money when everyone is supposed to pitch in to host an event when you know that you can help out.

- You show faortism to someone you have a crush on in the company despite their slacking, and lack of work ethic.

- You lie for your friends at work when they do something you know is wrong.

- You spend several hours a day using your work phone or computer during company hours and or disappear during the day to use them.

- You use up the last paper in the printer and fail to replace it leaving the task to the next employee who uses the printer.

- You hoard supplies at your desk so that you won't run out while other employees go without supplies they need to do their work.

- You gossip about other employees.

- You tell a potential customer that your company provides a specific service but you're not really sure that it does.

- You fail to do something important that you were asked to do and instead of doing it or letting someone know, you just hope that the higher ups don't notice or don't make a big deal about it.

- You act as if you were the only person who who contributed to a body of work. You take all of the credit or down play their role.

The scenarios surrounding these occurances I've mentioned can happen to any of us every once in a while. However, if these are habitual occurances, it might mean that you lack integrity.

I have learned that just like we all are wise in some areas of life but foolish in others, in the same way, we have more integrity in some areas than we do in others. We might think ourselves to be people of high integrity; however, in reality we have more integrity when more is on the line. I have also observed that some people are the opposite; displaying more integrity with shallow issues than they do with weightier issues.

SIGNS THAT YOU'RE IN AN ENVIRONMENT SUFFERING FROM UNETHICAL LEADERSHIP

Sometimes we can be oblivious to the fact that we're in an unhealthy and unethical work environment. In some instances, the worker is so enthralled with the idea of working for the company or the specific boss that they ignore the tell-tale signs that there are unethical decisions being made even on a daily basis.

1. **Harrassment Complaints**: Harrassment is a staple in unhealthy and uneathical work environments; even when the organization is supposed to be founded by "ethical" figureheads.

2. **Stealing**: Stealing is another staple. When an environment is truly honest and transparent, what you will find is employees bringing things TO the office, rather than taking things away. In an ethical environment, people are taught to ginuwinely have honor and show that

honor towards one another. There is a deep conviction to treat others as they would want to be treated.

3. **Fighting**: Where there is a lack of morals, there you will find bickering, petty arguments, a lack of cooperation, sabotaging, a lack of team work and even fist fighting.

If you happen to find that you're in an unethical work environment there are some options to consider. Leaving is always an option. However, you must consider all the risks involved. You must take a hard look at your financial circumstance and exercise caution. Talk to someone you trust about it. Make it a matter of prayer. Weigh the pros and cons involved but beware that when you decide to stay in an unethical environment, you're choosing the consequences aswell. They may not be honest with you and your future at this place is in question. You probably will end up being mishandled in some way eventually. Also remember this, "Be careful the environment you choose for it will shape you; be careful the friends you choose for you will become like them." ~ W. Clement Stone

Signs that YOU are an Unethical Leader

There are many unethical leaders in every type of organization. It is crucial that all leaders habitually examine themselves to ensure that they are making the decisions that are best for their workers. Here is a list of signs that you might lack integrity in leadership.

- **A lack of trust from your subordinates**: People aren't as naïve as they can sometimes seem. Within us all is a little voice that tells us that someone isn't right. The problem is that some people ignore that voice and this is why people are deceived. When you're an unethical leader, your subordinates have a sense that they cannot trust you and the result of which means that they're slow to act upon what you ask them to do because they aren't sure if they're doing the right thing by obeying you. They try to cover themselves and they will consult with other authorities to make sure that they're doing things ethically or how to go about it instead of just running with what you told them to do. There is uneasiness that people feel around you and this leads to hesitency.

- **You're self centeredness**: Unethical leaders are narcissist. They believe it's all about them. They lose sight of the vision and how it serves people because their focus is about what will get them selves ahead. They struggle to empathize with those around them because if it doesn't directly affect them, it doesn't move them. They look out for them selves and if that means throwing people under the bus, they will. If that means someone else will be hurt or inconvenienced because of their actions, it's not a big deal.

- **You're numbers oriented**: It doesn't matter to you that the results you expect are unrealistic. You push, threaten and belittle your employees for not producing but you don't consider that they might be understaffed, lack supplies and or resources to complete the project.

- **You rationalize breaking the rules to get something done**: Cutting corners and doing things you aren't supposed to just so that you can accomplish what you want can lead to a host of unethical actions and practices and eventually they are found out and resented.

- **The opinion of your subordinates means nothing to you**: When your subordinates complain to you, you ignore them, over talk them and dismiss them all together but when you have a complaint, it's made loud and clear and you demand obedience.

- **You hold others back to suit your own needs**: Though as a leader, you are looked up to by those around you for assistance with getting ahead, you make it a point to discourage someone from leaving if you will lose something because of it. Instead of promoting them, you hold them back until you're ready to release them even if it's in their best interest to proceed.

- **You're careless and don't think ahead:** Because you are numbers oriented and unethical, you skip the important things during the process. So whatever you do has "holes" in it. These holes are made known later on during inopportune times or in review. This is because you lack the foresight and patience necessary to do things right.

- **You're stubborn:** This means that you're probably not open to doing things differently. This makes it hard for anyone to help you. You almost punish those who reach out to you because you're so defensive. Everytime someone offers you constructive criticsism, you see it as a form of attack. So you gain nothing from it.

- **You try to do everything yourself:** In your mind, the only time anything is done right is if you do it. If you were an ethical leader, there might be some truth in this perception but when you're an unethical leader, you want your hands in everything for two reasons, to maintain control and because you're paranoid. You don't trust that others will do things the way you'd want them done and the way you like to do this is by any means necessary. You also don't trust others because you're not trustworthy. This often means skipping over important issues that come up, overlooking details and or expecting unrealistic results.

- **You're only doing enough to get by:** Unethical leaders eventually stop trying. They get rusty and sloppy because they don't continue to sharpen their skills or stay relevant. This is because of the "know-it-all" attitude or grandiose thoughts of themselves that most unethical leaders share. You think you've already mastered whatever was needed to learn how to do what you do.

- **You lie to cover things up or to get things done**: When you cut corners, skip over the details, have unrealistic goals etc, things will start to fall apart but because an unethical leader is too proud to admit wrong doing, they will almost always lie about or gloss over their mistakes. Though they are very harsh when someone under their authority makes a mistake.

If you're an unethical leader, it's important for me to note here that I wasn't always an ethical leader either. I started to lead at an early age and I've learned a lot through trial and error. Hypocrisy made me blind to the mistakes I was making and how it was affecting my reputation. This is why I felt I had a responsibility to enlighten others in this respect to ethical leadership as there is a lot to learn on the topic however, not enough teaching on it in my view.

The Need For Ethical Leaders

According according to a recent survey of 1,000 workers across the country sponsored by Michelle McQuaid, an expert on workplace relationships, only 38 percent of those polled described their boss as "great," while 42 percent said their bosses don't work very hard and close to 20 percent said their boss has little or no integrity.

Additionally, the survey revealed that 36 percent of employees are happy at their job and 65 percent believe a better boss would make them happier, while 35 percent say a bigger paycheck would.

Close to 60 percent of Americans said they would do a better job if they got along better with their boss, and more than half (55 percent) think they would be more successful.

"This current situation in the workplace is taking an incredible personal toll on employees and for organizations, it is costing $360 billion a year in lost productivity," McQuaid said.

Day 1

The ethical leader invests in becoming equipped to lead.

"Give me an understanding heart so that I can govern your people well and know the difference between right and wrong. For who by himself is able to govern this great people of yours?" ~Solomon (1 Kings 3:9)

People who truly have the heart of a leader desire to learn how to lead properly. They're more interested in being equipped to lead, than they are with appearances. This is because they have true self-confidence. When a leader is truly confident, they invest in their own character and personal development. Leaders who lack confidence put on false airs to overcompensate for a lack of depth and competence. An ethical leader would use the resources available to them to grow so that they can better serve the people under them.

Day 2

The ethical leader knows how to protect their reputation.

Whoever walks in integrity walks securely, but he who makes his ways crooked will be found out."

~King David (Proverbs 3:9)

It's very important to remember that you cannot live apart from your personal brand. Everything you do, you do as you. It's hard to hide things in this day and age due to technology. So leaders must be especially careful about truly being a living example of the things they teach and claim to believe. If a leader fails to live congruently with their professed beliefs, eventually it'll come out and tarnish their image and possibly damage their influence. A leader is someone to be looked up to. Every leader should model the same level of integrity in their personal lives as they do on the job.

Day 3

The ethical leader has the charater traits required to lead effectively.

"Successful leadership is not about being tough or soft, sensitive or assertive, but about a set of attributes. First and foremost is character." ~Warren Bennis

I've met some good few educated people with very little people skills. They weren't taught the importance of character, morals, values, social skills, soft skills, etc; but they're very knowledgeable about their jobs. A genius couldn't even be effective in a corporate environment without social skills. Every leader needs to invest in understanding and dealing with people. It's not enough to have a great set of skills. Any business or organization requires teamwork. No one can do it all by themselves. Eventually you will have to deal with people and if you don't know how to, your efforts and knowledgability won't amount to much.

Day 4

An ethical leader takes credit for what goes right and what goes wrong under their watch.

33% of executive's time is spent responding to crises or problems.
--The Creative Group, July 2005

You can't take credit for what's right but blame others for what has gone wrong. I have learned that it's impossible to correct every little thing that's wrong in any environment no matter how excellent the leader is or how good their practices are. That's why it's called "work". It's never done. It's alright to admit when you haven't gotten around to addressing an issue as long as it's a legitmate priority on your list and you're actively seeking to improve that area. You cannot enhance anything that you refuse to acknowledge or take accountability for. Also, when you model not taking accountability infront of your subordinates, they'll do the same to you. You must model the behavior that you would like your employees to follow. Do NOT throw them under the bus.

DAY 5

The ethical leader sees their position as a calling not a job.

"Leadership is action, not position."

~Donald H. McGannon

The glamour associated with true leadership is short lived. It's like marriage in some ways. There is a "honeymoon" phase. You have to make the choice to stay "faithful" to your commitment to your calling if you're going to assume a leadership position. This means that you have to actively invest in it in order to see the results you long to see. It's not always easy and there will be ups and downs but when you feel that you've been selected to lead for a purpose, that purpose will motivate you to keep moving forward. Ethical leadership means taking your time to do things the right way, even when the wrong way is easier and faster. It means going the extra mile. It requires compassion and dedication but most of all a 'sense of destiny" (an inner knowing that you're supposed to be here for a reason). This is the driving force behind ethical leadership.

Day 6

An ethical leader seeks mentorship and accountability.

69% of business leaders say it's important to have a mentor.
--Grant Thornton's View newsletter, December 2005

Mentorship is essential to great leadership. There is no such thing as ethical leadership without a mentor. There must be someone that you can look to concerning major decisions. There must be someone who is modeling excellence in leadership in your life. There must be someone to help you stay accountable. It's best to have more than one; preferably three. When it becomes harder and harder for you to maintain your integrity, you need someone there to ensure that you are keeping things in proper perspective. The key to being the best leader you can be is surrounding yourself with individuals who are more intelligent and righteous than you are.

Day 7

An ethical leader teaches their subordinates how to invest in their character.

A leader is one who knows the way, goes the way, and shows the way. ~John C. Maxwell

It is important that you train your people in character and ethics and encourage them to do so on their own. Make it a top priority in the work environment. Don't ever make the assumption that they already know or that they should know better. I have found that it is never profitable to assume that someone has integrity. If you want something as important as ethics to be the center of your department, business or organization, you must take it upon yourself to facilitate the meetings in which this training takes place.

Day 8

An ethical leader is a trusted leader.

The glue that holds all relationships together - including the relationship between; the leader and the led is trust, and trust is based on integrity. ~Brian Tracy

People don't typically have a problem with heeding those they trust. You must build rapport with your subordinates. However, you must refrain from becoming too familiar with them. Earn their trust but do not allow yourself to become overly involved in their affairs unless the situation calls for immediate intervention; this is to protect yourself. A leader who is too familiar with their subordinates will receive the same results as an untrustworthy leader, delayed obedience. There must be a balance to your interaction with your workers.

DAY 9

The ethical leader has integrity... i.e. nothing to fear... and nothing to hide...

"The supreme quality for leadership is unquestionably integrity. Without it, no real success is possible, no matter whether it is on a section gang, a football field, in an army, or in an office." ~Dwight Eisenhower

Everyone accepts integrity. It's like honor. No one would reject it. Integrity simply means doing and saying exactly what you would do and say if the people your actions and words affected were present. The thing I love about integrity is that it relieves me of any stress of trying to hide something I've said or done. There is a freedom in leading and living with integrity but integrity is such a big word and it means so many things. It's important that you magnify the importance of the meaning of integrity to your people.

DAY 10

Ethical leaders are learners.

"Leadership and learning are indispensable to each other." ~John F. Kennedy

A leader should never stop learning. They should always seek ways to not only enhance their skillset and remain knowledgeable but also to stay relevant and engaged. When you fail to continue to educate yourself, you're setting yourself up to become despensible. Staying knowledgeable keeps you up on your toes and a valued part of the team. Knowledge increases your necessity and uniqueness. It makes you irreplaceable and more of a vital asset to the team. Don't get sloppy.

DAY 11

The ethical leader can handle criticsism and resentment.

"A man who wants to lead the orchestra must turn his back on the crowd." ~Max Lucado

Criticism, rensentment, and contempt come with the burden of leadership. You have to have tough skin and not allow your ego to be offended. You must learn how to distinguish between constructive criticsism and grumbling and complaining. Expect your subordinates to talk behind your back, curse you in secret, resent you, etc; but I would suggest that you address any blatant contention or dishonor and try to resolve such matters amicably but keep in mind that you will never be able to resolve all of these instaces and you shoudn't be moved or loose sleep over it. If you are generally loved, respected, admired and appreciated by the general consensus, these small matters will usually resolve themselves.

DAY 12

An ethical leader masters and teaches the art of transparency.

"The keys to brand success are self-definition, transparency, authenticity and accountability."

~Simon Mainwaring

Success means stress and stress can lead some people to want to hide things that they shouldn't. There must be a system of transparency and both you and your employees must master it to survive and thrive. Transparency brings accountability to people who are less than accountable. There are some people who are used to just doing whatever they want without having to answer to anyone. For that reason, though on paper they might be qualified, they aren't able to fulfill their duties properly. They have no accountability because they haven't been taught to hold themselves accountable. They need to be taught by you. As the leader, it's your responsibility to train your leaders on the practices of your organization.

Day 13

An ethical leader consistently promotes unity and consistently promotes the vision of the organization.

Leadership is the art of getting someone else to do something you want done because he wants to do it.
~ Dwight D. Eisenhower

At the end of the day, there must be teamwork. Without unity, projects and assignments will fall apart repeatedly. This type of problem will eventually cause the brand to have a bad name due to inconsistency. So from the first, there must be a sense of unity and community among the workers. They mustn't just "get along". They must see each other as valuable assests to the vision of the company/organization. However, none of your employees or volunteers can get on board with a vision they don't properly understand. As the leader in the environment, the purpose, passion and ultimate goal must continually be communicated through speeches, lessons, and even in pictures. Set the tone for inspiration and you'll see a change in the people who work for you.

DAY 14

An ethical leader is authentic.

A common trait of great leaders is honesty.

~Aimee Colbert

An unauthentic leader produces unauthentic subordinates. Lead by example. Your subordinates are following you. They will become like you. You have to examine yourself and ask yourself if you're being as authentic as you possibly can be. Are you being true to yourself and to your people or are you patronizing them? I have noticed that the less authentic a leader is in his dealings with his workers, it sends a subliminal message to those workers to be unauthentic also. Without sincerity, your workers won't work their best and you won't be able to trust them.

Day 15

An ethical leader knows that the people are more important than the "system".

"You have to treat your employees like customers."

~ *Herbert D. Kelleher*

Every business and organization is really all about one thing; the people. But you have to care about the people WITHIN the organization/business and not just the people you're selling to. Being a leader takes wisdom. Not every situation is black and white. Therefore, the system in which you do things can fail you. It's important to follow your policies but the policies were made to serve the people who serve you. It gives an order to serving those people in return. If your policies cause you to do a disservice to your own people, that system needs to be updated or it's not being used properly. Think of King Solomon's wise decision. He could have followed protocol but it would have not issued the proper justice. So as a leader, you must discern how to properly render justice to those under your authority.

Day 16

Ethical leaders do not see themselves as authorities but as the voice of authority.

A leader should not desire to be revered as a God. They are to become the mouth piece of God, not pretend to be Him. They aught to say what God would say without expecting people to figurateively bow down and worship them.

~ Aimee Colbert

There are some people who seek the position of leader because they want things their way. They love for people to serve and fear them. An ethical leader leads the people because of his compassion for the people. He has a vision. He has a mission and he is determined to see the people through to their goal. An ethical leader also answers to a higher authority. Are you using your position as an opportunity to serve or to be served? Are you spending more time making demands than you are encouraging and training your workers?

Day 17

An ethical leader is admired and obeyed.

If you command wisely, you'll be obeyed cheerfully.
~ Thomas Fuller

Some leaders are admired but not obeyed and some are obeyed but not admired. This is the difference in ethical leaders. An ethical leader has admirable qualities but that doesn't mean that he is a push over that is bent on winning the approval of his subordinates. Leaders must convey a level of seriousness and firmness that will help motivate their workers to work efficiently. There must be consequences. Also, expectations must be made known through reviews and progress reports. An ethical leader does not blame their workers for not obeying. They carry out the consequences according to their offenses and those consequences speak for themselves when talking is no longer enough. Being consistently firm is sometimes all it takes to set unmotivated workers on the right track. Do your workers admire and obey you?

DAY 18

An ethical leader's values are visible on a daily basis.

Example is leadership. ~ Albert Schweitzer

It's one thing to voice what you believe as a leader but it's another thing to live it and to live it on a consistent basis. A leader has to master maintaining his countenance because his countenance decides the flow of the environment. Your subordinates shouldn't fear talking to you because they discern that you're in a bad mood… again. Every leader needs a positive outlet, affirmations and coping skills. Every leader also needs to learn how to keep home matters at home. Is it hard for you to keep your emotions in check on the job? Keep in my that you must practice what you preach and not make excuses for yourself.

Day 19

An ethical leader feels that it's important for their workers to have time to enjoy their families.

A man should never neglect his family for business.
~ Walt Disney

In my observations, I perceive that visionaries have one major thing in common. They want everyone to respect their time but they don't respect the time of their workers. They don't care that they call their workers on their off days to come in. They don't care that they take their holidays away. They don't care that they keep them home late from their families and they don't care if those families are falling apart because of them. I have always seen leaders be resented for this reason. It has never sat right with me. Sometimes the bosses are so wrapped up in their goals that they forget about their own families and expect their workers to do the same as a sign of devotion to the company; more like worship to me. People are not machines. Ethical leaders don't manipulate their workers that way.

Day 20

An ethical leader is approachable.

An unapproachable leader is a resented leader.

~ Aimee Colbert

Have you ever noticed that your workers become quiet and intimidated when you walk by? It might be because you're not approachable. If so, renetment is in your near future if it's not there already. An ethical leader has an open door policy, not a "do not disturb" policy. Leave your door open. Listen to your worker's concerns. Smile more. Let them see you laugh out loud. Have regular one-on-ones. Interact more. Solve problems. This is how you let your workers know that you're available, accessible and won't mind getting to know them.

Day 21

> An ethical leader empathizes with an employee who desires a raise.

The task of the leader is to get his people from where they are to where they have not been.
~ Henry A. Kissinger

An ethical leader doesn't hesitate to help those seeking a raise to become equipped to receive one. The quality of living your staff member has should mean something to you. If you can't look upon your staff members with compassion, you cannot make ethical decisions about their pay. You will make decisions based upon what is best for you at the expense of your workers. I have seen some unethical leaders even give gifts or bonuses to their workers to distract them from the fact that they aren't being paid enough even when the business is doing well. It's true that some workers feel that they deserve raises when they actually don't. This is when you help them to work their way up to deserving the raise but never dismiss their attempts to get one. Equip them with the resources they need to earn their raises.

Day 22

An ethical leader doesn't throw their workers under the bus when they are the ones who made the mistake.

"In too many workplaces, when something goes wrong, people waste far more time and energy assigning blame for it than trying to find a solution," ~ Ben Dattner

It is so easy to blame workers for something that goes wrong rather than properly equipping them to handle the task you've asked them to undertake. I have seen leaders do this and it's so unfair. They expect unreasonable results but they don't supply their workers with the things they need to get the job done, then when things go wrong they blame them. Blaming is unethical in itself but to blame someone for the consequences of your lack of assistance is grossly distasteful. Accept accountability for when you screw up or your subordinates will never accept responsibility for the wrong they do cause.

Day 23

An ethical leader doesn't show favortism.

James 2:9 But if you show partiality, you are committing sin and are convicted by the law as transgressors.

One thing I have seen unethical leaders do in order to manipulate their workers is to show partiality. They do this in order to provoke them to jealousy and lead them to compete with one another. They make the one they show favor to a target by doing so and eventually, cause their workers to resent each other. This ultimately blows up in their faces because it slows productivity. People will stop working together and start to argue instead. They will end up sabotaging each other and the company will fail. Ethical leaders praise good work and reward those who not only produce in numbers but also those who show great character.

Day 24

Ethical leaders are convicted by the thought of their subordinates having to live on little pay.

Employees who believe that management is concerned about them as a whole person - not just an employee - are more productive, more satisfied, more fulfilled. Satisfied employees mean satisfied customers, which leads to profitability. ~ Anne. M Mulcahy

One of the quickest ways to lose the respect of your workers is to convey that you don't care whether or not they have enough money to live on. There are times when departments have to cut back, lay people off or downsize. This is common but what should never be expected or accepted is the idea that it doesn't matter whether or not people receive their proper pay, bonuses, over-time and any other monetary compensation they're due or how they'll survive. If cuts must be made, there should be a plan in place to recover. There should also be cooperation for those trying to make up for less pay and they should not be punished or resented for seeking supplemental pay elsewhere.

Day 25

An ethical leader is enjoyable.

People buy into the leader before they buy into the vision.
~ John C. Maxwell

It's important to be likeable. It's not enough to be knowledgeable. It's not enough to be the best. You have to be pleasant to get the best out of your workers. Show them that you have a sense of humor. Compliment your staff. Stop being so insecure. Be flexible. Use your manners. Be humble, friendly and empathetic. This way, your workers will do their best because they don't want to disappoint you.

Day 26

An ethical leader criticizes performance but praises the performer.

Affirmation without discipline is the beginning of delusion. ~ Jim Rohn

Praise is essential to potential. Leaders must know how and when to praise the efforts of their workers. People will always pursue pleasing the person who is the source of their encouragement. You must become that person. There's no easier way to boost morale in an office than to throw out a few compliments here and there. Make it personal and not always general. Go to specific people to let them know how valuable all of their work has been. Praise those who might feel overlooked. Those are the high risk workers who must continually be reassured. They need to hear you say that they matter to you. Learn how to do that without making that employee a target of envy. Do you compliment your workers enough?

Day 27

Ethical leaders creates a positive and happy environment.

Outstanding leaders go out of their way to boost the self-esteem of their personnel. If people believe in themselves, it's amazing what they can accomplish.
~ Sam Walton

The atmosphere has to be conducive to the results you want to produce. People work better in happier environments however it's no easy task to maintain and protect such an environment. Leaders have to be on their guard against anything that causes a disruption of peace. They also have to have the forsight needed to prevent such disruptions. Every leader must learn how to protect the peace within their environment and that means taking the time out to address any major office related conflicts instead of just letting it work it self out. I personally believe that every environment needs a protocol for complaints that is easy to understand and follow. These steps will help to maintain order if followed correctly.

Day 28

An ethical leader nurtures their subordinates and helps them to overcome their problem areas.

Leadership is unlocking people's potential to become better. ~ Bill Bradley

An unethical leader has no concept of nurturing. All that matters to them is numbers. When they don't see the numbers they want, they punish or fire people. An ethical leader knows how to discern the weaknesses of their workers, assist them, train them, teach them and re-position them according to their true abilities until they can truly fulfill their roles. Even if the leader doesn't have the time to nurture said worker, they'll put them with someone they can trust to handle the issue. Do you know how to properly assess your workers? Do you make it a priority to assist them in enhancing their skills?

DAY 29

An ethical leader doesn't promote someone into a position unless and until they're ready for it.

A premature promotion leads to premature decisions.

~ *Aimee Colbert*

I think that one of the worst mistakes a leader can make ever is to promote someone who isn't ready for a position or doesn't deserve it. It not only causes resentment in the office but it also leads to a variety of complaints. Some leaders promote certain workers in order to prevent them from finding a job elsewhere. It's like putting an engagement ring on someone you don't really want to marry just to prevent them from breaking up with you. The problem is that this leads to more problems than solutions. "Potential" is also not a good enough reason to promote someone. Babies have potential. Prisoners have potential. Promotion is only deserved unless and until that person has overqualified for their current position.

Day 30

An ethical leader is patient and understanding.

Unfortunately, I have seen more men attempt to become leaders than I have seen men attempt to learn how to lead.

~ Aimee Colbert

One of the problems that most unethical leaders have is a lack of patience and understanding. Most founders have studied their trade; their passion but not their people. They understand laws, practices, business, marketing, etc… but they lack in people skills. This is why they usually find someone else to run their companies for them. It's hard to have to interact with people on a daily basis and running the ins and outs of a business but anytime you embark on building a brand, you must also embark on understanding and dealing with people. Have you invested in learning how to manage and deal with people ethically? How you ever pursued leadership training?

Day 31

An ethical leader is teachable and values constructive criticsism.

Working at Pixar you learn the really honest, hard way of making a great movie, which is to surround yourself with people who are much smarter than you, much more talented than you, and incite constructive criticism; you'll get a much better movie out of it. ~ Andrew Astanton

Every leader should be easy to talk to. You never want people to dread bringing a problem to you nor should you punish them for telling you their truth. I say "their" truth instead of THE truth because sometimes the "truth" they bring is based on assumptions. Whether what they're saying is true or not, allow people to feel comfortable with having a calm and rational discussion with you. The more untouchable you seem to be, is all the more people will hold things in and eventually blow up on you at an unopportune time or leave you without an explaination.

CONTACT THE AUTHOR

WWW.aimeecolbert.Com

WWW.Facebook.Com/Dr.AimeeColbert

WWW.Twitter.Com/AimeeTweets4U

CHECK OUT THESE OTHER TITLES:

- The Drama Free Life
- The Irreplaceable Man
- The Irreplaceable Woman
- I Survived
- Time Out!
- Peace Be Still
- I'm Just Sayin

Now available on Amazon! Type in keywords "Aimee Colbert"

www.ingramcontent.com/pod-product-compliance
Lightning Source LLC
Chambersburg PA
CBHW051820170526
45167CB00005B/2094